Contents

A Message from ABBA

Isn't it amazing how quickly time seems to pass! It doesn't seem a year ago that we were welcoming you to our last Annual, but the calendar tells us it certainly has been that long.

First of all, we'd like to thank you for your appreciation of last year's Annual. The only regret we have about it is that apparently, some of you were disappointed because you were unable to get a copy before it sold out, and we're very sorry about that, and have done our best to ensure that the same thing doesn't happen this year.

As it's the end of another fantastic year for us (and of course, we owe our success to you, our faithful fans), we're planning for next year, and hoping that we can continue to provide music that will appeal to you. It's a little too early to say exactly what will be happening for us, but as usual, we'll be trying to appear on television as often as we can.

Now it's time for us to get back to some of the other things which constantly seem to be piling up. Thank you for buying this Annual (and although we seem to say this every year, this one really does seem better than ever to us), and our grateful thanks for your continued support. In the words of the song on the 'Super Trouper' Album — 'Happy New Year'.

ABBA

On and on and on...

Well, certainly that's the title of one of the more recent brilliant songs by the most successful foursome of all time in the field of popular music, but it also seems a nice way to describe the incredible progress made by that same foursome during their career together of just about eleven years by the time you're reading this. Yes, it was in November, 1970, that the four friends who had all made their mark as popular singers and musicians in Sweden first performed together in public, although they weren't called Abba in those far off days. In fact, at that point the four had no idea of what the future would hold for them — what happened was that Benny Andersson and Bjorn Ulvaeus were performing as a duo, and were booked to appear in a restaurant in Gothenburg on the South West coast of Sweden. Benny was engaged to Anni-Frid Lyngstad, Bjorn was engaged to Agnetha Faltskog, and neither of the girls, although they too were in the entertainment business, was working that evening. What could be more natural than that they should decide to help out their loved ones on stage? The name they chose to describe this group, which was only intended as a one night joke, indicates the light hearted way in which the whole event was treated — the soon-to-be fab four called themselves the Festfolk Quartet, and in case you might be wondering, 'Festfolk' can either mean 'engaged couples', fiancés, if you like, or 'party people'.

You're probably thinking that this was the first step on the ladder to international fame and worldwide acclaim, and if this was a fairy story, that's exactly what should have happened. But this is no fantasy, this is the story of Abba, and after what was reportedly a disastrous debut (caused by the fact that the songs the quartet chose to sing, although most appropriate for a performance in a restaurant, were of no interest to the people who were performing them), the idea of forming a group was nearly forgotten for ever, and it took nearly two more years, a period which included another not too successful show in Gothenburg, before any more progress could be made on the road to forming the group whose music we all enjoy so much.

In fact, the four people who later became Abba had experienced some success together, although only as a recording group, as opposed to being a full time live act. Benny and Bjorn had begun to write songs together, several of which became hits as recorded by Benny's old group, the Hep Stars. They had also written and recorded 'She's My Kind Of Girl', released under the name of Benny and Bjorn, which had become a hit in Japan, and on this song, the girls had helped them out, although they weren't credited on the record label. Early in 1972, the quartet also featured together in a song which Benny and Bjorn had been invited to submit as an entry for a Japanese Song Festival, 'Santa Rosa' and a few months later, all four again were involved in the first American release by Benny and Bjorn, 'People Need Love', although the girls were credited under the name of Svenska Flicka — you can hear the song on that incredible Abba Album, 'Greatest Hits', by the way. The Abba magic was definitely in evidence even then, although their name was still a few months from being conceived...

In 1973, Benny, Bjorn and their manager, Stig Anderson, were invited to write a song which would be considered as a possible Swedish entry for that year's Eurovision Song Contest. By this time, it had become obvious that the song would be performed by Bjorn, Benny, Agnetha and Frida, and in fact that was the name which appeared on the sleeve of the album whose title was also the name of the song which Bjorn, Benny and Stig wrote for the Swedish Eurovision heat, 'Ring Ring'. The most peculiar part of this particular story has to be that 'Ring Ring', although it was the overwhelming favourite of just about every person in Sweden, was only placed third in the Swedish competition because the decision as to who would represent that country in the Eurovision Contest proper was left to a panel of so called 'musical experts'. When they didn't recognise Abba's song as far and away the best in 1973, the public outcry in the media saw to it that, from that point on, Sweden's Eurovision entry was chosen by ordinary people.

It was around the time of this controversy that Stig Anderson, who was continually referring to the quartet when talking to newspapers, came up with the abbreviation Abba, using the initial letter of each person's name — just think, it might have turned out to be FABB (Frida, Agnetha, Benny, Bjorn), but fortunately Frida's full first name is Anni-Frid! Since then, there have been numerous instances of other people using the name Abba, many of them illegally — Abba are very proud of their name, and don't want it applied to anything which they haven't personally sanctioned through Polar Records headquarters in Stockholm, Sweden — but there had also been two instances of the name Abba being used before it was used by this great group. One abba (with a small 'a') was an American songwriter who was active around the time of the Second World War, while the other Abba was the name of a Swedish fish canning company, but there's not much doubt who's the most famous Abba around now, is there?

Since those days nearly nine years ago, a great many things have happened to Abba, most of them entirely beneficial. From being a well-known act in Sweden and one or two other neighbouring countries, the group have spread their wings, scoring hit records in almost every country in the world, the only notable exception being China — but as Bjorn said, "I don't think they have too many record players there, do they?" The group has won gold, silver, and platinum awards for gigantic record sales in dozens of different countries over six continents, they've appeared before several royal families, and they've taken part in a television broadcast seen by an estimated three hundred million people (that was the 1979 'Save The Children' concert for the benefit of the United Nations Children's Fund, by the way). In Britain alone, Abba have scored more top ten hits during the period from the spring of 1974 (when 'Waterloo' became their first top tenner and first number one) than any other act, and almost inevitably, they've had more number one hits than anyone else as well. Advance orders for their albums have continually set new records (if you know what we mean) — when 'Arrival' was released in 1976, the figure was three hundred thousand advance sales, and three years later, when 'Greatest Hits Volume Two' came out, twice that number of people had put in their orders before release date. Even more recently, when 'Super Trouper' hit the shops, more than a million Abba fans had placed their faith in Abba before hearing the album, and we're absolutely sure that there was very little disappointment, if any, when those million people first heard the magic of tracks like 'Our Last Summer', 'The Winner Takes It All', 'Super Trouper' and 'On And On And On' — and that's how it goes with Abba. On and on and on, with more and more admirers in more and more places, fans aged from seven to seventy and beyond. This is the age of Abba, and it's difficult to imagine any of us getting tired of their amazing music, so let's hope they continue to go — on and on and on...

ABBA

First Lines

Each of the phrases listed below is the first line of a song by Abba. What do you have to do? Simple — just work out which song each of the lines belongs to...

1. No more carefree laughter _KNOWING ME KNOWING You_
2. When you were lonely _____
3. I'm nothing special _THANK YOU FOR THE MUSIC_
4. No smiles, not a single word at the breakfast table _____
5. If you change your mind _TAKE A CHANCE ON ME_
6. The summer air was soft and warm _____
7. I was at a party _on and on and on_
8. People everywhere _____
9. Last night I was takin' a walk along the river _ANGLE EYES_
10. Lay your head on my chest _____
11. Soy muy sencilla_____
12. I'll never know why I had to go _____
13. They came flyin' from faraway _EAGLES_
14. The city is a jungle _TIGER_
15. They came from the hills _THE PIPERS_

12

ABBA
The Hit Process

Records are so much taken for granted these days that it's often forgotten that a great deal of hard work goes into preparing them for release. Obviously, the song has to be written, then it has to be arranged before it can be recorded. After that, the recording has to be mixed into stereo (recording is usually done in studios which can record up to 48 tracks separately, and all these have to be compressed together to produce two track stereo) and the mixed recording mastered to produce a metal 'stamper' which can be used to press the track onto the vinyl of which records are made. Then there's the design of a sleeve, labels, and so on — it's quite a lengthy business!

Abba, or more particularly Benny and Bjorn, are experts at the recording process, which is the area we'll be concentrating on here. Without any of the processes mentioned above being carefully undertaken, the Abba record you buy would be less than perfect, but it's quite obvious that the actual capture of the sound of instruments and voices is one of the most crucial phases. For various reasons, Abba try to work in the studio on weekdays only, and between the hours of ten a.m. and ten p.m. — "That leaves the weekends free for us to be with our children, and working through the night, as some artists seem to prefer, would mean that we would be asleep all day and out all night, which wouldn't be very nice for our families". Bjorn and Benny also like to have completed the writing of each song before they attempt to record it — obviously, this is an advantage in that valuable studio time is not spent building a song up from a faint idea, and as Abba are such perfectionists in making sure that every word in the lyric is perfectly appropriate, and that musically, the backing tracks are as good as they can possibly be, many hours could be spent with little to show for them at the end.

With the song written to their satisfaction, Benny and Bjorn go into the Polar Recording Studio. Before May 1978, the group had found it necessary to book time in several other Swedish studios, but because studios throughout the world are in great demand, sometimes suitable studio facilities couldn't be found, and this put unnecessary pressure on the group, especially at a point when they were in a hurry to complete an album. As a result, Polar decided to build a studio on which the label's artistes and principally Abba, could have first call. (Of course, Abba are not always recording, and from time to time, Polar Studios are not required by Polar artists, so that the studio can be used by others — a measure of how excellent its facilities are is that such notable British stars as Led Zeppelin and Mike Rutherford and Tony Banks, both members of Genesis, recorded very successful albums there).

A most essential element in a successful studio is the engineer, and Abba have a genius working for them in the Polar Studio, Michael B. Tretow ('Micke' for short). Micke had worked with the members of Abba on numerous projects prior to being chosen to work in their own studio, among them solo LPs by Agnetha and Anni-Frid, and even with the Hootenanny Singers, Bjorn's early band, so that he was an obvious choice. Once Benny and Bjorn have played a rough 'demo' of a song to Micke, they begin to prepare a backing track of purely music, usually with their regular backing musicians, guitarist Lasse Wellander, bass player Rutger Gunnarsson and drummer Ola Brunkert (you can read about this amazing trio elsewhere in this annual). Benny plays keyboards, of course, and Bjorn, although he may play some acoustic guitar from time to time, works very closely with Micke to make sure that every note of music is recorded correctly.

When the basic backing track is complete, there may be a requirement for another instrument to be added to the slowly growing recording — a saxophone, perhaps, or a string section, and these are recorded next, although on separate tracks so that nothing which has previously been perfectly recorded is spoilt by the additions. When that phase is over, and a full backing track has been satisfactorily completed, it's time to begin recording the vocals. As Benny said, "Only when we're sure that the backing track is spot on do we begin to think about the voices, and we have to build them up gradually by overdubbing" (adding more and more often identical vocal lines) "until the harmonies are complete. We have to be careful to ensure that we don't end up with something which sounds amazing on record, but which we can't reproduce live — it would be very embarrassing to have to refuse to perform a song because we knew we simply couldn't match up to the recorded version".

So it's not until many hours have been spent on instrumental recording that Anni-Frid and Agnetha are invited to the studio to record their vocal parts, although, as Benny is at pains to point out, "They do pop in the studio occasionally before the vocal sessions to see how things are turning out, and often the ideas they have are used in the final version of a song which appears on record". When the vocals are complete, the next phase is mixing, which can take much longer than might be thought — every instrument has to be at the correct recording level so that, for example, the drums don't drown everything else, and the singing has to be clearly audible, but not to the point where the listener can't really hear the carefully crafted backing track. It's an enormously lengthy and time-consuming business, making records — for example, making 'The Winner Takes It All' involved perhaps two days preparing the backing track, another two days when the girls supplied their vocals, and maybe even longer to finalise the mix. As Benny says, "It's really all in the mixing. That's what can take the time, but it's also what can make a song sound great". And 'great', as we all know, is exactly what Abba's records definitely sound...

ABBA's Views

This is how Abba feel about some interesting aspects of their lives

ON TELEVISION

"I watch more television when I'm in England, but when I'm at home, I try to watch at least one news programme a day, and maybe a good film if there's one on" **(Agnetha)**

"Agnetha used to say that I was a TV addict, but that's not really true. Actually, the mention of television always makes me think of Los Angeles, because of all the stations there are to choose from. It's incredible—you can watch a cartoon at five o'clock in the morning" **(Bjorn)**

ON BOOKS

"I'm a science fiction fan and have been for many years. I find nothing more relaxing than to lean back with a good book, so I read as much as possible. My favourite authors are Nevil Shute, Harry Harrison, John Steinbeck..." **(Benny)**

ON FOOD

"I'm very fond of health foods, but I try to mix things up because they can be boring sometimes. I eat a lot of salads and I love Italian food — pastas and spaghetti. When I'm at home and doing the cooking, I mostly cook things like that" **(Anni-Frid)**

ON CLOTHES

"I like wearing jeans and pullovers, clothes I can feel comfortable in. My favourite colours for clothes are blue and white, although I do enjoy clothes that are red and black, and I prefer boots to shoes" **(Agnetha)**

"I'm not all that interested in clothes, though I'm glad we don't have to wear flashy stage costumes very often. Nobody ever bothers to ask my opinion about stage outfits, because they know I'm not much use at that kind of thing. I just like to be comfortable and look all right" **(Benny)**

"That's something that really interests me. I'm very aware of fashion and I keep in touch with new trends through magazines, talking to designers, and, of course, through looking round shops. I like to think of myself as being fashion-conscious without being a slave to fashion" **(Anni-Frid)**

ON FILMS

"All the good films tend to come out at once, but one film I loved was 'Close Encounters', I remember. I've got lots of favourite actors and actresses, but maybe as far as actors go, I enjoy Richard Burton and Jack Nicholson, and some of my favourite ladies on the screen are Vanessa Redgrave, Ellen Burstyn and Julie Christie" **(Benny)**

I'm a science fiction freak especially, but I like most kinds of films except those French and Italian love stories where everyone talks all through the film and nothing ever happens" **(Bjorn)**

"I like going to the movies, and I enjoy all kinds of films, but I think Roman Polanski is my favourite director. I've got so many favourite movie stars — Burton and Taylor, Liv Ullman, Jack Nicholson, and there are lots more" **(Agnetha)**

ON MUSIC

"The kind of music I like depends very much on my mood, but I like most kinds if I'm in the right frame of mind. Soul is my favourite popular music, and I've listened to a lot of opera on the classical side" **(Anni-Frid)**

"Music is a very large part of my life. I listen to records a great deal, every kind of music except modern jazz. I like lots of classical composers, but particularly Mozart, Bach, Beethoven and Tchaikovsky, and I'm very keen on Fleetwood Mac and Stevie Wonder as far as pop goes" **(Benny)**

"I like many different classical composers — Bach, Brahms, Mozart and Beethoven, among others. I try to hear as much new pop music as possible, so we get all the new American and British chart entries sent to us each week, so that we can keep up with what else is happening. I wasn't too keen on punk rock — some of it did have a certain energy, but it's not really my kind of music" **(Bjorn)**

ABBA WORD SEARCH

Here's the latest Abba word search, but it's a word search with a difference — every word you have to find (and they're all listed below) can be found on the cover or inner sleeve of the magnificent 'Super Trouper' LP. We don't need to tell you who recorded that, do we? Good luck!

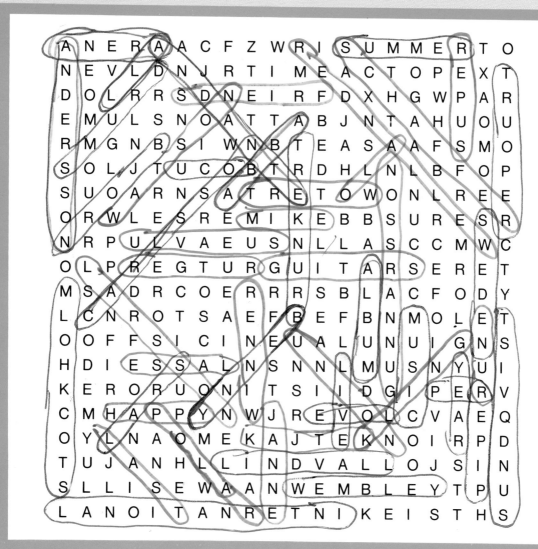

```
A N E R A A C F Z W R I S U M M E R T O
N E V L D N J R T I M E A C T O P E X T
D O L R R S D N E I R F D X H G W P A R
E M U L S N O A T T A B J N T A H U O U
R M G N B S I W N B T E A S A A F S M O
S O L J T U C O B T R D H L N L B F O P
S U O A R N S A T R E T O W O N L R E E
O R W L E S R E M I K E B B S U R E S R
N R P U L V A E U S N L L A S C C M W C
O L P R E G T U R G U I T A R S E R E T
M S A D R C O E R R R S B L A C F O D Y
L C N R O T S A E F B E F B N M O L E T
O O F F S I C I N E U A L U N U I G N S
H D I E S S A L N S N N L M U S N Y U I
K E R O R U O N I T S I I D G I P E R V
C M H A P P Y N W J R E V O L C V A E Q
O Y L N A O M E K A J T E K N O I R P D
T U J A N H L L I N D V A L L O J S I N
S L L I S E W A A N W E M B L E Y T P U
L A N O I T A N R E T N I K E I S T H S
```

And these are the words you're searching for:

ABBA	GUITARS	LOVE	SUPER
ALBUM	GUNNARSSON	MIKE	SWEDEN
ALL	HAPPY	MUSIC	TRETOW
ANDANTE	INTERNATIONAL	OLA	TROUPER
ANDERSSON	JANNE	PER	ULVAEUS
ARENA	KAJTEK	PIPER	UNION
BENNY	KLING	POLAR	WATSON
BJORN	LARS	RUNE	WELLANDER
BOCU	LARSSON	RUTGER	WEMBLEY
BRUNKERT	LASSE	SCHAFFER	WINNER
CARLSSON	LAST	STOCKHOLM	YEAR
DRUMS	LINDVALL	SUMMER	
FRIENDS	LIVE	SUNDQVIST	

19

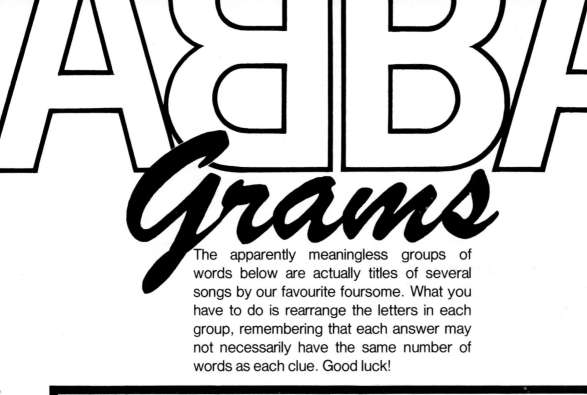

ABBA Grams

The apparently meaningless groups of words below are actually titles of several songs by our favourite foursome. What you have to do is rearrange the letters in each group, remembering that each answer may not necessarily have the same number of words as each clue. Good luck!

1. Blank Cord Lorn _Rock'n Roll Band_
2. Eleven Pole Dope _____
3. Bleary Anna In Triplet _____
4. Pure Sure Port _SUPER TROUPER_
5. Ace Make None Chat _TAKE A CHANCE ON ME_
6. Washingtons Trite Fifth _____
7. If So Risk Fees _____
8. You Learn Loom Valley _____
9. Frayed Dish Wend Loot _____
10. Trail Winkle East Then _THE WINNER TAKES IT ALL_
11. Why Yen Appear _HAPPY NEW YEAR_
12. Mouse Slur Tram _____
13. Maria Note Time _____
14. No Mean Moon Anew _____
15. Heavy White Tomb Died _____

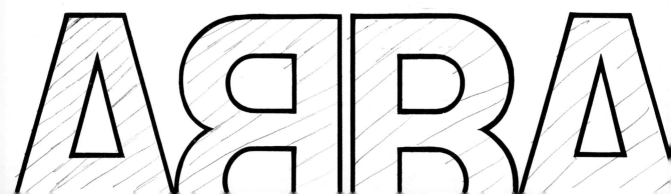

ABBA Spoof

Here's a game for two people using our favourite letters of the alphabet — we're sure you've already guessed that those letters are 'A' and 'B'! All you need to play the game is two pieces of paper (or preferably cardboard) for each player, These are known as tiles, and each tile needs the letter 'A' written on one side of it, and the letter 'B' on the other (see below)

Object of the game

To make the word ABBA — each player places his two tiles on the table, keeping them covered with his hand, having first decided which combination of letters he wants to play (i.e. two 'A's, two 'B's, or one 'A' and one 'B'). After deciding who will start the game by spinning a coin, the first player calls 'ABBA', and both players uncover their tiles: If the letters displayed make up the word 'ABBA', the first player scores one point. This continues, with the same player starting each time until the displayed letters show some combination other than 'ABBA', when the other player becomes the caller. Only the player who calls 'ABBA' can score, and the winner of the game is the first to score twenty points. Once you've played the game for a few minutes, you'll undoubtedly find that trying to predict which letters your opponent will choose is rather more difficult than it may seem!

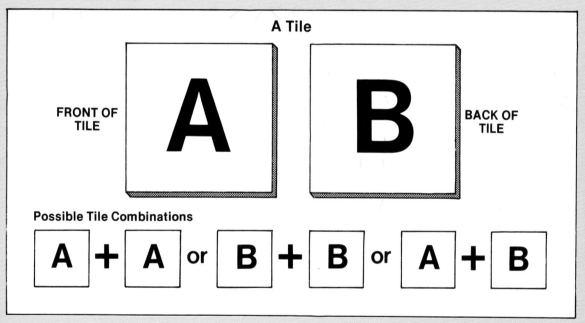

A Tile

FRONT OF TILE **A** **B** BACK OF TILE

Possible Tile Combinations

A + A or B + B or A + B

Scoring Combinations

FIRST PLAYER		SECOND PLAYER	
A	B	A	B
A	A	B	B
B	B	A	A

Non-scoring Combinations

To score a point, two letter 'A's and two letter 'B's must be visible. Therefore, any other combination (i.e. four 'A's, four 'B's, three 'A's and one 'B', or three 'B's and one 'A') fails to score.

The U.K. ABBA

'Waterloo'

(Epic EPC 80179)
Released: May 17th, 1974

'Abba'

(Epic EPC 80835)
Released: June 7th, 1975

'Greatest Hits'

(Epic EPC 69218)
Released: March 26th, 1976

'Arrival'

(Epic EPC 86018)
Released: November 5th, 1976

'Abba — The Album'

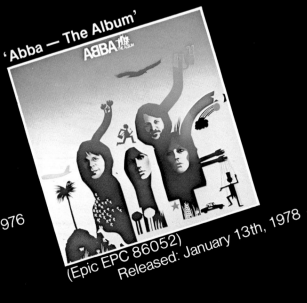

(Epic EPC 86052)
Released: January 13th, 1978

Album Collection

'Voulez-Vous'

(Epic EPC 86086)
Released: May 4th, 1979

'Greatest Hits Volume Two'

(Epic EPC 10017)
Released: November 2nd, 1979

Lining up for another Platinum disc presentation. Benny spoofing again!

'Gracias Por La Musica'

(Epic EPC 86123)
Released: August 27th, 1980

'Super Trouper'

(Epic EPC 10022)
Released: October 31st, 1980

ABBA

Cover Versions

Vera Lynn

Abba's Songs Recorded by Other Artistes

You're probably quite familiar with the term 'cover version', but if you're not, it means another version of a familiar song performed by someone entirely different from the originator. Now there are certain songwriters whose songs have been 'covered' by dozens, perhaps hundreds, of other people — the Beatles, or rather John Lennon and Paul McCartney, are just one example of a writing team whose songs have been recorded by literally heaps of people.

You've probably guessed that this feature is to tell you about some of the versions of Abba's great songs which have been recorded by other people. Now we're certainly not telling you that any of these are better than the real Abba recordings, but if you should chance to run across any of these people's records in someone else's collection (or even in your own, which you may be unaware of!), you might just find it interesting to hear different treatments of the songs which you know so well. So here goes...

It's pretty obvious when you think about it that there's not much future in trying to outdo Abba at what they do best, so there haven't been that many vocal cover versions of Abba's songs. Who, after all, wants their work to be compared unfavourably with something which is almost inevitably superior? However, a few people have chanced their arm in this way, and some of the names make interesting reading. Vera Lynn, for instance, ended her hitmaking career as far as the charts go back, in 1952, but for many years before that, her name was guaranteed to sell records in vast quantities. You can probably tell from all that that Vera wouldn't be likely to record one of Abba's rockers, but what can be heard are her versions of both 'I Wonder (Departure)' and 'Thank You For The Music'. Staying with the ladies, would you believe that Abba's labelmates in Britain, the Nolans, or as they were called at the time, The Nolan Sisters, recorded 'Money Money Money' on their '20 Greatest Hits' album, and 'Thank You For The Music' on another of their LPs? Good taste, those girls...

The Nolans

Lena Martell, she of 'One Day At A Time' fame (and who also probably prevented Abba from scoring another chart topper with 'Gimme Gimme Gimme', by the way), recorded 'Hasta Manana' and 'I've Been Waiting For You', but that must have been some years ago, while the Ladybirds, who are best known as one of this country's best teams of lady backing vocalists, turned their hand to 'The Name Of The Game' and a prototype, but far less successful, version of the Nolans known as the Anderson Sisters seem to have been the only notable act to attempt a cover of 'Suzy Hang Around'. We should applaud their good taste in choosing a fine song, although even that didn't help them to make the charts.

By far the biggest number of Abba cover versions are by orchestras, who are naturally forced to concentrate on the music rather than the lyrics most of the time. In fact, more than one famous orchestra leader has devoted a whole LP to songs by Abba, including Frank Pourcel, whose LP includes versions of 'Hole In Your Soul' and 'Eagle', along with other more predictable

Abba originated hits, and Arthur Greenslade, who had the temerity to call his album 'Abba's Greatest Hits'! 'When I Kissed The Teacher' and 'My Love, My Life' were the less obvious covers on that record, but much more straightforward was the Alan Tew Orchestra's 'Abba Songbook' a full LP's worth including instrumental versions of the first five Chart toppers by our favourites. Other well known orchestras, like those of Joe Loss, Ray McVay, Geoff Love, Les Reed and Paul Mauriat, have also recorded one or more Abba classics, but perhaps the greatest accolade to the group in this area came when James Last, the German orchestra leader whose records sell in prodigious quantities, recorded four songs, including 'Fernando', 'Dancing Queen' and 'Knowing Me, Knowing You', on a double album titled 'Last The Whole Night Long'. If Abba were at all concerned by the royalties they make from cover versions (and we're sure they're not!), this album alone would put their bank manager's mind at rest!

A rather more curious phenomenon relating to cover versions is the fact that several Military Bands have recorded a good deal of Abba's material, most notably the Band Of The Life Guards, who released a 1978 LP titled 'On Parade With The Music Of Abba', and the Band of the Royal Corps of Transport, whose LP was called (of course!) 'Salute To Abba'. There are several other brass bands, like the Royal Scots Dragoon Guards (chart toppers in 1972 with their alarming version of 'Amazing Grace' — remember that?) who have chosen an Abba song or two to record, although it's certainly hard to imagine Benny and Bjorn writing songs designed to inspire the armed forces — but if the songs can do that, well, why not? Oh yes, and we mustn't forget the Brighouse and Rastrick Brass Band, another act which nearly topped the chart a year or two ago with their version of 'The Floral Dance', because they've recorded 'Take A Chance On Me'...

Mike Oldfied

However, it hasn't all been instrumentals, although one of the most famous Abba covers also comes into this field, the late 1980 version by 'Tubular Bells' superstar Mike Oldfield of 'Arrival' — Mike even used a helicopter on the picture sleeve of his single for added authenticity! Neither has it only been Europeans who've chosen Abba songs to improve their hit chances — the Boones, a family group made up of the children of 1950s megastar Pat Boone, have recorded 'Hasta Manana', and Latin American bandleader Edmundo Ros, as well as American lady singer Carol Douglas, have tried their hands at 'Waterloo'. Another act who made an entire album of Abba songs, Nashville Train, sound like they should be Americans, but it appears that 'Abba Our Way', released in 1979 on the rather obscure Buffalo label, is the work of a Swedish group! Very strange...

Abba fanatics will, of course, know that only one cover of an Abba song has ever entered the British charts, and that was 'Honey Honey', which made the top ten in 1974 in a version by Sweet Dreams. Of course, there could be plenty more cover hits in the future — in Ireland, a group called The Others had a top twenty hit with 'Ring Ring', proving, along with Sweet Dreams, that such things are definitely possible.

Then there's the School Choir of St. Winifred's, who hit big last year with 'There's No-One Quite Like Grandma' — they covered 'Dancing Queen' on an LP, as did the group who many people think copied everything about Abba (same line up, even winning Eurovision!), the Brotherhood Of Man...But one area of music which we've not covered here is the Rock scene — Abba's music certainly doesn't immediately suggest itself as a suitable vehicle for punk rockers or New Wavers, does it? Yet there have been at least two Abba songs played by groups from this field. 'S.O.S.' by a now defunct band from Nottingham known as the Favourites isn't really too good, although it seems, on hearing their attempt, that they were at least trying to be serious. Much more interesting is 'The Name Of The Game', a live version of which appeared on a single by the very promising Any Trouble. The band's leader and singer, Clive Gregson, starts the song off by saying 'This is a song by one of our favourite bands', and the version comes off rather well. I'm sure we all know exactly what he means!

James Last

ABBA

Okay, ladies and gents, it's time to put on your thinking caps and memory banks for the 1982 bumper Abba quiz. Ready? Off we go — eyes down and no cheating!

1. Name Abba's first eight number one singles in Britain — but make sure they're in chronological order!
2. Of their first twenty singles released in Britain, name the six titles by Abba which failed to reach the top three in the charts.
3. What are the full names of the four members of Abba?
4. Name the five American acts who are also featured on the 'Music For Unicef' LP along with Abba, and also name the song which Abba donated to the Unicef cause?
5. Following their 1979 tour of Britain, a member of Abba's backing group released a solo single in Britain. What was the record's title, and what was the artistes name?
6. The company which publishes Abba's music in Britain is called Bocu Music. The name 'Bocu' is made up of the first two letters of the surnames of two people — what were their full names?
7. Bocu Music also published a Eurovision winner by another artist in 1980. What was the song's title, and who sang it?
8. Another well known Swedish company uses the name 'Abba', apart from our favourite quartet. What business is this other company involved in?
9. In 1979, one member of Abba was given a non-musical role in a Swedish film. What was the film's title, in which country was it made, and who was the Abba person?
10. What were the names of the famous Swedish groups of which (a) Benny and (b) Bjorn were members before they formed Abba?
11. In 1975, Bjorn, Benny and Stig Anderson wrote a Eurovision song for another Swedish act. The song later appeared on the 'Abba' LP, but what was its title, and what was the name of the act?
12. What are the three songs which comprise the folk medley on the B side of Abba's 'Summer Night City' hit?
13. Two important Abba dates are April 6th, 1974, and January 9th, 1979. What happened on each of those dates?
14. During 1979/80, three LPs were recorded by British acts in Abba's Stockholm studio. Each of the resulting albums made the British chart — what were the names of the three acts, and what were the titles of their albums?
15. Where can you find the answers to (nearly) all these questions?

QUIZ

Across

1. Where the Abba success story began in Britain (7)
7. Second song in Abba's trilogy (1, 6)
11. Audiences would never do this to our favourite foursome (3)
12. - - - - the Terrible was a famous tyrant of the past (4)
14, 42, 68. - - and - - and - -, sing Abba (2, 2, 2)
15. This must be a strange country—Abba have only topped their charts once—so far! (3)
17. A brief trade mark (2)
18. Type of word describing something or someone (4)
20. A short American lawyer (2)
21. The opposite of AD when applied to years (2)
23. - - room at the inn, the Bible tells us (2)
24. American disco group who hit with 'I Want Your Love' (4)
26. Me, - - - - - -, I, sang Joan Armatrading (6)
28, 109 across. - - - - your Brother, an early Abba song (2, 2)
30, 70. Abba sang about sitting on one of these (4, 4)
33. Fall over by mistake (4)
35. This is the way out! (4)
36. Back to front, Abba rarely play this way — unfortunately for us! (4)
37. Does your mother do this, ask Abba? (4)
38. We feel very sorry for people who can't do this — it means missing great music (4)
39. See 32
41. In short, your family doctor (2)
42. See 14 across
43. How the French say 'we' (4)
46. A kind of jug (4)
49. Make sure you notice this abbreviation (2)
51. Sailing ships can't go far without this (4)
52. Our planet revolves around one (4)
53. -, -, D, C, B, A (2)
54. A beautiful blonde lady who's definitely still alive (7)
56. Forget me? I wouldn't! (3)
57. It's one of these that Abba are the greatest group in the world (4)
60. How the Germans say 'I' (3)
61. If at first you don't succeed, do this again (3)
63. Abba donated 22 to this cause (6)
65. Along with 76, this lady was good friends with Abba (5)
68. See 14 across
69. Donald Duck miniaturised? (2)
70. See 29 across
72. Small Royal Academy? (2)
74. Mr. Diddley or Miss Peep? (2)
75. Used to run (3)
77. You must do this if you don't want to be involved (5)
79. Swedish island where our favourite quartet often live (7)
80. See 66
81. Two year old musical fashion short for modern (3)
82. Chinese Chairman (3)
83. Kisses — Fire, one of many Abba classics (2)
85. This is how you feel when you're not well (3)
86. A type of Buddhism (3)

89. Originally an item of male apparel, now a unisex upper garment (5)
92. The label on which the best group in the world appear (4)
94. Teacher's initial comment after good work (2)
95. They're on sale everywhere, but we've still never seen one with fingers! (4)
96. Abba's right hand lady assistant (5)
98. - - - Trouble, a group who've covered one of Abba's biggest hits (3)
99. Wet floor? Use this to dry it (3)
100. Do this in pain if you stub your toe (4)
103, 1 down. One of Abba's ever faithful drummers (3, 8)
104. If your're 84, you do this (3)
105. You get this by multiplying length by width (4)
106. Your guests stay in a spare one of these (4)

CROSSWORD

10. A small Rolls Royce (2)
13. - - More Heroes, a Stranglers hit (2)
14. A precious stone (4)
16, 65 **down**. Abba's only non-hit single in Britain (2, 4)
19. Six of these were a hit for both Major Lance and Wayne Fontana (2)
20. You can do this on Abba's records to be great (6)
22. It may be unlucky for some, but this was Abba's thirteenth British hit single (10)
25. If you annoy someone, you do this to them (3)
27. A chap listening for thunderous noises in an Abba hit (8)
29. In both Latin and French, this means 'and' (2)
30. This, with a squared radius, results in 105 (2)
31. The way you address your old friend Algernon (4)
32, 39. Abba's second British number one (5, 3)
34. A superior quality of this sort of music is what Abba produce (3)
38. Two of these were an album track here and an Abba single hit in America (5)
40. A beautiful dark lady from a wonderful group (8)
44. Meaty cubes make good gravy (3)
45. The final letters of this clue — but don't guess! (2)
47. Opposite of 14 across (3)
48. Geste, Brummel or Bridges? (4)
50. Tooting - - - a London underground station (3)
51. Where Napoleon capitulated, but Abba broke through (8)
55. Old fashioned way to address a relative (4)
58. Initially, the Campaign for Nuclear Disarmament (3)
59. Rivers which are this flow into the sea (5)
62. A single for Abba, but also an album title (6, 4)
64. The Jam sang about rifles from here (4)
65. See 16
66, 80. Side One, Track Three of the 'Abba' LP (8, 8)
67. A hit title shared by Abba and Roxy Music (5, 4)
71. Precede this with a 't' and you have Abba's stablemates (2)
73. If you want some help, you require this (3)
74. Put this in front of a word, and it implies a pair (2)
76. One of Abba's friends, who's married to 65 (4)
78. A large tub of liquor (3)
81. On which the cat sat? (3)
82. Married to Mrs., perhaps (2)
84. What Abba receive for playing a concert (3)
87. Shortly, for example (2)
88. After following this man, Abba dance beneath the moon (5)
89. This follows a coconut at a fair (3)
90. Eskimo accommodation (5)
91. Abba's Swedish record company (5)
93. This can also be called a pigtail (5)
95. What golfers shout when their ball might hit someone (4)
96. English title of the song which was runner up to Abba at Eurovision (2)
97. Tried to get there quickly, although on foot (3)
99. There are lots of these in an atlas (3)
101. Make a mistake (3)
102. Reed or Christie? Both hitmakers (3)
107. Diminutive Member of Parliament (2)
109. Why did - - have to be me, ask Abba? (2)

108. Before a word, this means against it (4)
110, 111. Abba's eighth British LP (5, 7)
112. You break into this before you gallop (4)

Down
1. See 103
2. Our little kingdom (2)
3. The Eagles sang about one in California (5)
4. - - - Robinson, hitmaker with '2-4-6-8 Motorway' (3)
5. Summer - - - - - - City, another Abba hit single (5)
6. - - - - - - - Queen, a chart topping smash for you know who (7)
7. Hole - - Your Soul, a rocker from 'The Album' (2)
8. With the mouth (4)
9. One of these hands does things well (3)

33

While there can be no doubt that much of the magic of Abba is due to Agnetha, Benny, Bjorn and Anni-Frid, it's equally clear that Abba have a number of very special people who also contribute strongly to the group's international success. Stig Anderson is one name that comes immediately to mind—the man who has made sure that everything which bears Abba's name (including this very annual!) is worthy of their approval. Stig's responsibilities are far too many to list here, but they run from the group's music on one side of the spectrum to their investments on the other. Then there's Micke Tretow, upon whose experience and expertise Abba rely when they're in the studio, Thomas Johansson, who organises tours, and Claes af Geijerstam, who mixes Abba's live sound, not to mention our very own John Spalding, who looks after Abba's British interests, as well as being heavily involved in Abba's international activities.

The Stars Behind the Stars

On this occasion, however, we're going to concentrate on three stalwarts of Abba's backing group. These are the men who have to produce in the studio and on stage the sounds which Benny and Bjorn require, and that's not such an easy task, as Abba music is as close to perfection as anyone else's in the world. The trio of 'faithful retainers' (although they're not nearly as old as that phrase might indicate) are drummer Ola Brunkert, bassman Rutger Gunnarsson and Lasse Wellander, 'Abba's own guitar hero', as he's called in 'Abba For The Record'.

ABBA

Ola Brunkert started playing drums as long ago as 1958 (!), although he obviously wasn't very old at the time. "I had a band at that time together with some friends who lived nearby. I was very influenced at the time by a jazz drummer named Gene Krupa, and so we started off playing New Orleans styled jazz". And if you can recall 'I Am The Beat' by The Look, a big hit in early 1981, that song mentions Gene Krupa...Ola's introduction to Abba came back in 1973, after they heard his work with their fellow Polar artist, Ted Gardestad—Benny and Bjorn had obviously played with numerous drummers before, so

it was quite a compliment to Ola when he was invited to appear on the sessions for the 'Ring Ring' album, and since then, Abba have very rarely used anyone else as their rhythmic backbone, although Roger Palm has occasionally deputised when, for one reason or another, Ola has been unavailable. Ola, you see, makes his living as a session musician, and says he prefers it that way, and wouldn't be happy to be in the limelight as much as the four Abba principals. Although he finds himself playing several different types of music each week, Ola enjoys working with Abba more than any of his other work—who wouldn't? It must be an enormous buzz to know that you're working on a song which will be heard by hundreds of millions of people all over the world...

Ola's regular rhythm section partner since Abba first achieved worldwide fame has been bass playing virtuoso Rutger Gunnarsson. In fact, the bass wasn't Rutger's first instrument—when he was twelve, he began to learn guitar, although it wasn't with a view to performing with rock bands, as he was more interested in classical music, and defined his playing as 'similar to that of Julian Bream or John Williams, but not as good!''. Curiously, the main reason for Rutger's change to bass guitar was because he felt lonely and exposed playing classical guitar —in the more serious musical fields, guitar is mostly treated as something which functions without any other backing instruments.

Rutger soon joined a rock band as bass player, and ran across the Hootenanny Singers, a group of which Bjorn was a member, of course. As well as being an excellent player on his chosen instrument, Rutger has an extra string to his bow which Abba have often found it convenient to use —he's also a very good arranger of music, and wrote the string parts for 'The Album', for example, and is also well-known for his horn arrangements, which makes him very much 'in demand' in his native land as a session player with other special accomplishments. Rutger has appeared on every Abba album since the pre-Abba 'Ring Ring' LP, and there seems no reason to suppose that he won't be around for some time yet... And then there's the great Lars 'Lasse' Wellander. Lasse is the player whose name most people will probably recognise of the three featured here, but oddly enough, he has been with Abba for less time than Ola or Rutger. Lasse started learning guitar during the early 1960s, his motive being that it was a craze among his friends in his small home town of Nora, which is about 170 miles from Stockholm. Of course, at that time the Beatles were making world headlines, and influencing people all over the world to learn the guitar—a lot of the time, this was a passing phase, although not for Lasse, who remembers forming a 'group' with the boy next door when he was twelve years old. "We used to amplify our guitars through an old radio, and play songs that were in the top ten, but unfortunately, most of the time we were playing entirely different chords from those we should have been playing!''. Later on, of course, Lasse tought himself to play the right chords, and reckons that it was a great help also playing accordian.

For both the 'Ring Ring' and 'Waterloo' albums, Abba used Janne Schaffer as their lead guitarist, but once again, it was as a result of playing with Ted Gardestad that Lasse attracted Benny and Bjorn's attention, although he was taken on 'the staff' a little later than Ola Brunkert, who met Abba in the same way—that's no reflection on Lasse's playing, by the way, but rather because Abba are lucky enought to be able to call on two world class guitarists in Lasse and Janne, both of whom continue to work with the group from time to time, although Lasse is currently the 'main man'. In fact, the two have fairly different guitar styles— on the 'Voulez-Vous' album, Lasse plays on 'Chiquitita', for example, while Janne plays on the title track.

As influences on his playing, Lasse feels that blues players from some years ago have been significant in his own progress as an axeman, and also names Eric Clapton as a major influence. While he has played on numerous sessions besides those for Abba records, Lasse also has his own group, along with Mats Ronander (the other guitarist on the 1979 tour), and from time to time, Rutger Gunnarsson is also a member of the group, when his other commitments allow. Just like Ola and Rutger, though, Lasse is very happy playing with Abba and remaining out of the spotlight. Maybe that's a necessary attribute for any musician invited to play with Abba—but there are, of course, some amazing compensations!

United States of America

(all Abba's singles in the U.S.A. are released by Atlantic records)

Titles	Catalogue number	Release date
Waterloo/Watch Out	3035	May 1974
Honey Honey/Dance (While The Music Still Goes On)	3209	Aug 1974
Ring Ring/Hasta Manana	3240	Dec 1974
S.O.S./Man In The Middle	3265	June 1975
I Do, I Do, I Do, I Do, I Do/ Bang-A-Boomerang	3310	Dec 1975
Mamma Mia/ Tropical Loveland	3315	May 1976
Fernando/Rock Me	3346	Aug 1976
Dancing Queen/That's Me	3372	Nov 1976
Knowing Me, Knowing You/Happy Hawaii	3387	April 1977
Money, Money, Money/ Crazy World	3434	Sept 1977
The Name Of The Game/ I Wonder (Departure)	3449	Nov 1977
Take A Chance On Me/ I'm A Marionette	3457	April 1978
Does Your Mother Know/Kisses Of Fire	3574	May 1979
Voulez-Vous/Angeleyes	3609	Aug 1979
Chiquitita/Lovelight	3629	Oct 1979
Chiquitita/I Have A Dream (Spanish version)	3630	Oct 1979
Gimme, Gimme, Gimme/ The King Has Lost His Crown	3652	Feb 1980
Winner takes it all/Elaine	3776	Nov 1980
Super trouper/The piper	3806	Apr 1981
On & On & On/Lay all your love	3826	Jun 1981

GREAT BRITAIN

(All Abba's singles in Britain are released by Epic Records)

Titles	Catalogue number	Release date
Ring Ring/Rock'n Roll Band	EPC1793	Oct 1973
Waterloo/Watch Out	EPC2240	April 1974
The Music People At Eurovision (EP-1 track by Abba	EPC2283	April 1974
So Long/I've Been Waiting For You	EPC2848	Nov 1974
I Do, I Do, I Do, I Do, I Do/ Rock Me	EPC3229	July 1975
S.O.S.(Man In The Middle	EPC3576	Sept 1975
Mamma Mia/ Tropical Loveland	EPC3790	Nov 1975
Fernando/Hey Hey Helen	EPC4036	Mar 1976
Dancing Queen/That's Me	EPC4499	Aug 1976
Money, Money, Money/ Crazy World	EPC4713	Nov 1976
Knowing Me, Knowing You/ Happy Hawaii	EPC4955	Feb 1977
The Name Of the Game/ I Wonder (Departure)	EPC5750	Oct 1977
Take A Chance On Me/ I'm A Marionette	EPC5950	Jan 1978
Waterloo/Watch Out (reissue)	EPC5961	Feb 1978
Fernando/Hey Hey Helen (reissue)	EPC5962	Feb 1978
Summer Night City/ Folk Medley	EPC6595	Sept 1978
Chiquitita/Lovelight	EPC7030	Jan 1979
Does Your Mother Know/ Kisses Of Fire	EPC7316	April 1979
Voulez-Vous/Angeleyes	EPC7499	July 1979
Gimme, Gimme, Gimme/ The King Has lost His Crown	EPC7914	Oct 1979
I Have A Dream/ Take A Chance On Me	EPC8088	Dec 1979
The Winner Takes It All/ Elaine	EPC8835	July 1980
Super Trouper/The Piper	EPC9089	Nov 1980

Singles Discography

West Germany

(All Abba's singles in West Germany are released by Polydor Records)

Titles	Catalogue number	Release date
People Need Love/Merry-Go-Round	2041 369	1972
Ring Ring/Rock'n'Roll Band	2041 422	April 1973
Ring Ring/Wer In Wartesaal Der Liebe Steht	2040 105	Aug 1973
Waterloo/Watch Out	2040 114	Mar 1974
Waterloo/Watch Out (German version)	2040 116	April 1974
Honey Honey/Ring Ring	2040 120	June 1974
So Long/I've Been Waiting For You	2040 131	Nov 1974
I Do, I Do, I Do, I Do, I Do/Rock Me	2001 579	Mar 1975
S.O.S./Man In The Middle	2001 585	July 1975
Mamma Mia/Intermezzo No. 1	2001 613	Nov 1975
Fernando/Tropical Loveland	2001 639	Mar 1976
Dancing Queen/That's Me	2001 680	July 1976
Money, Money, Money/Crazy World	2001 696	Oct 1976
Knowing Me, Knowing You/Happy Hawaii	2001 703	Feb 1977
The Name Of The Game/I Wonder (Departure)	2001 742	Oct 1977
Take A Chance On Me/I'm A Marionette	2001 758	Jan 1978
Eagle/Thank You For The Music	2001 778	May 1978
Summer Night City/Folk Medley	2001 810	Sept 1978
Chiquitita/Lovelight	2001 850	Jan 1979
Chiquitita/Lovelight (Spanish version)	2001 874	April 1979
Does Your Mother Know/Kisses Of Fire	2001 881	April 1979
Voulez-Vous/Angeleyes	2001 899	July 1979
The Winner takes It All/Elaine	2001 989	July 1980
Super trouper/The piper	2002012	Nov 1980

AUSTRALIA

(all Abba's singles in Australia are released by RCA Records)

Titles	Catalogue number	Release date
Waterloo/Watch Out	102436	April 1974
Ring Ring/Rock'n'Roll Band	102496	Aug 1974
Honey Honey/Dance (While The Music Still Goes On)	102514	Sept 1974
Waterloo EP	20605	Oct 1974
So Long /Hasta Manana	102560	Dec 1974
I've Been Waiting For You/King Kong Song	102561	Dec 1974
I Do, I Do, I Do, I Do, I Do/Rock Me	102607	April 1975
Mamma Mia/Hey Hey Helen	102671	Aug 1975
S.O.S./Man In The Middle	102690	Sept 1975
Fernando/Tropical Loveland	102746	Feb 1976
Dancing Queen/That's Me	102814	July 1976
Money, Money, Money/Crazy World	102835	Sept 1976
Knowing Me, Knowing You/Happy Hawaii	102870	Jan 1977
The Name Of The Game/I Wonder (Departure)	103006	Oct 1977
Take A Chance On Me/I'm A Marionette	103050	Jan 1978
Eagle/Thank You For The Music	103130	May 1978
Summer Night City/Folk Medley	103202	Sept 1978
Chiquitita/Lovelight	103297	Feb 1979
Does Your Mother Know/Kisses Of Fire	103350	May 1979
Chiquitita/Lovelight (Spanish Version)	103359	June 1979
Voulez-Vous/Angeleyes	103414	Aug 1979
Gimme, Gimme, Gimme/The King Has Lost His Crown	103452	Oct 1979
I Have A Dream/Take A Chance On Me	103551	Feb 1980
The Winner Takes It All/Elaine	103645	Aug 1980
On & On & On/The piper	103719	Nov 1980
Super trouper/Happy New Year	103747	Mar 1981

These releases are up to date at the tume of going to press.

The Supreme Compliment

It doesn't take a 'Mastermind' champion to know that lots of books have been written about lots of pop stars, and Abba are no exception, as most of you will already know. But there is one great compliment which has been paid to Abba which is only shared by a very few of the world's supergroups, and that's a book that is album-sized, a book that will fit in your record collection right next to your Abba LPs.

You might think that it's not so special, but because of the technical aspects of book publishing, to put together a book that is roughly thirty centimetres square is not something which happens too often, because it creates production problems and is actually much more expensive than printing a normal book. The obvious question must then be 'Well, why bother?'', and the answer goes something like this... The most popular and famous artistes not only work for long periods on the recording of their LPs, they also work very hard to ensure that, when a record arrives in the shops, it looks as good and as appetising as it possibly can. That's why the sleeves on your Abba albums are often works of art on their own account, and can be appreciated, if necessary (but let's hope it never is necessary!) without listening to the records they contain. If you turn to the centrefold of this annual, you'll certainly see what we mean... In a book about a group as famous as Abba, it would be quite simple to provide miniaturised photographs of their LP sleeves, but this doesn't allow those reading the book to appreciate every detail. Added to that, there are some very beautiful pictures of Abba which we've all seen, although usually printed fairly small — with an album-sized book, these great photographs can be printed at larger than normal size, which makes them all the better. That that should give you the idea...

Before the publication of 'Abba For The Record', the only stars who had been paid the compliment of such large books were The Beatles, The Rolling Stones and Bob Dylan — just about the only acts who can hope to compare with Abba in terms of record sales and popularity (and we hear that there will soon be a similar volume on the subject of David Bowie). 'Abba For The Record' is the most complete history of our favourite group, and contains numerous photographs from the private collections of the members of the group, as well as a detailed chronological account of how Anni-Frid, Benny, Bjorn and Agnetha got to the point where they decided to form the greatest group in the world, and the successes they achieved as Abba. The book was written by John Tobler, who seems well qualified for the task, as he was Abba's first press representative in this country, and actually worked with Abba when they won the 1974 Eurovision Song Contest with a sparkling performance of 'Waterloo'. That's described in 'Abba For The Record', as is everything in which the group has been involved since then.

Well, that's not quite true, because 'Abba For The Record' documents the Abba story in some detail, but only up to the end of 1979. Since then, there's been two whole years of Abba activity, including a tour of Japan, number one singles like 'The Winner Takes It All' and 'Super Trouper', plus the 'Super Trouper' album, the Spanish LP—lots of exceedingly interesting activities, which aren't at the moment covered in 'Abba For The Record'. But here's the good news — John Tobler is working on updating 'Abba For The Record', probably just about the time you're reading this, and some time during the New Year, you'll be able to buy the new, thicker, updated edition, which John promises will be even better than his first great work. "Some time during 1982" is the closest we can get John to predict a date for publication of the revised edition, but more definite news will be published in the 'Abba Magazine' when a certain publication date becomes known. It wouldn't be a bad idea to start saving up now!

ABBA WORD SEARCH

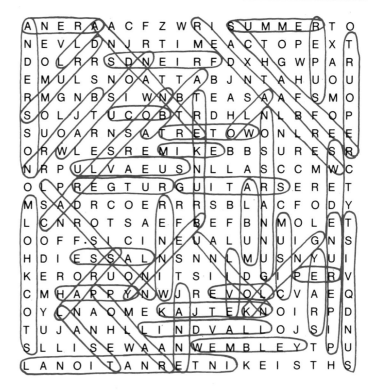

ABBAGRAMS

1. Rock'n Roll Band
2. People Need Love
3. Nina Pretty Ballerina
4. Super Trouper
5. Take A Chance On Me
6. If It Wasn't For The Nights
7. Kisses Of Fire
8. Lay All Your Love On Me
9. The Way Old Friends Do
10. The Winner Takes It All
11. Happy New Year
12. Our Last Summer
13. I'm A Marionette
14. One Man One Woman
15. Why Did It Have To Be Me

FIRST LINES

1. Knowing Me, Knowing You
2. Why Did It Have To Be Me
3. Thank You For The Music
4. One Man, One Woman
5. Take A Chance On Me
6. Our Last Summer
7. On and On and On
8. Voulez-Vous
9. Angeleyes
10. Kisses Of Fire
11. Gracias Por La Musica (Spanish version of 'Thank You For The Music')
12. As Good As New
13. Eagle
14. Tiger
15. The Piper

44

ABBA QUIZ

1. 'Waterloo', 'Mamma Mia', 'Fernando', 'Dancing Queen', 'Knowing Me, Knowing You', 'The Name Of The Game', 'Take A Chance On Me' and 'The Winner Takes It All'.
2. 'Ring Ring' (twice), 'I Do I Do I Do I Do I Do', 'So Long', 'Summer Night City' and 'Does Your Mother Know'.
3. Anni-Frid Synni Lyngstad-Andersson, Goran Bror Benny Anderssson, Agnetha Ase Faltskog, Bjorn Christian Ulvaeus.
4. Earth, Wind and Fire, Donna Summer, John Denver, Kris Kristofferson, Rita Coolidge. Abba's UNICEF song is 'Chiquitita'.
5. The song was 'Not Bad At All' (which was a pretty accurate title), and the singer was Tomas Ledin.
6. H. Elton Box and Ivor Cutler.
7. 'What's Another Year', sung by Johnny Logan.
8. Canning fish.
9. The film was 'Walk On Water If You Can', it was shot in Spain, and Anni-Frid played a small part.
10. (a) The Hep Stars and (b) the Hootenanny Singers.
11. The song was 'Bang-A-Boomerang', and Sven and Lotta sang it in the Swedish Eurovision heat.
12. 'Pick A Bale Of Cotton', 'On Top Of Old Smokey' and 'Midnight Special'.
13. April 6th, 1974, was the day Abba won the Eurovision Contest, and January 9th, 1979, was the date of the Music for Unicef concert.
14. Tony Banks (of Genesis) made 'A Curious Feeling', Mike Rutherford (also of Genesis) made 'Smallcreep's Day' and Led Zeppelin made 'In Through The Out Door'.
15. 'Abba For The Record', of course—haven't you got your copy yet?

Ratings

We reckon that makes fifty possible correct answers, and this is how we rate the various scores achieved.

50 correct. Excellent. You are undoubtedly an ace Abba fan, and we recommend that you enter for 'Mastermind'. Well done!

40-49 You probably know more about Abba than 99% of the group's fans. It surely wasn't the last question in the quiz that you failed on!

31-40 You're probably a newcomer to the wonderful world of Abba, and if that's the case, you've done very well, and next year, you'll be much nearer a maximum.

21-30 Oh dear. We'll have to assume you've been on a very long holiday to Mars or the Moon.

Below 20 We are absolutely speechless!

GIANT CROSS WORD

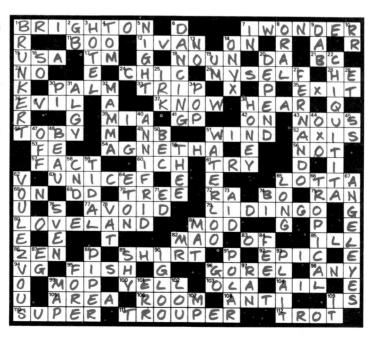